piercing the long night

ARTHUR GINSBERG

for my grandchildren
Aden, Griffin, Isabeau and Nia

History says, Don't hope
On this side of the grave…
But then once in a lifetime
The longed -for tidal wave
Of justice can rise up,
And hope and history rhyme
… Seamus Heaney

CONTENTS

ONE

IX

Election 2016   1

Baked In   2

Labor Day 2016   3

Broken 2017   5

Beheaded on TV   6

Amnesia   8

Lies   9

Lured   10

Capitol Blues   12

I Can't Breathe   13

Memorial Day 2019   15

Storm   16

Marjorie Stoneman Douglas   17

Rushmore, July Fourth, 2020   18

Corgi Congress   20

Election 2020   21

Exeunt   22

Caviar   24

Transition Blues   25

Look!   26

Seascape   27

Contempt   28

On a Perspective of Things   30

Why   31

Ukraine   33

Something Beyond   35

Eggs   36

Blank Canvas 37

Kite 39

The Flow of Being 40

The Tyranny Of 41

Hope 42

Subtraction 43

Reunion 44

Blood 46

At the Psychiatrist's Office 47

The Drowning Pool 50

Homage to the Heart 52

Inviolable 53

To Our Knees 55

Quarantined 57

Easter Sunday 2020 59

Masking 61

Contactless 63

Down the Road 65

Art in the Time of Covid 67

T W O

69

Diptych 70

After Jack's Heart Attack 72

Hot Tub Man 73

The End of Jack 75

Farewell W D Clay 76

Cemetery 77

Batman Lego 79

Encounter 80

Looking Back in the Rearview Mirror 81

Koons, Poons & Cattelan 83

Epiphany 85

Cancer 86

Silent Signals 88

Murmuration 89

For the Dearly Departed 90

Introspection 92

Afternoon Practice 94

The Falls 96

Walking with Mozart 97

Zoo 98

X-mas Heart-string 100

Digging for Worms 101

Deep Freeze 102

Bald Eagle 103

Moss 104

Frog 105

Rhapsodic 106

Pine Cones 107

Come Late Summer 2020 108

Dear Hawthorn 109

The Pineapple Express 110

Life in the Balance 112

Skellig Michael 114

Valentia Island Cottage in the Rain 116

Backpack 117

The Cairn 119

Rocky Mountaineer 120

Hiroshima Peace Park, 2017 122

Icelandia 124

Nostalgia, Cannon Beach, 2018 126

Cannon Beach Sonnet 127

Piercing the Long Night 128

ONE

Election 2016

Winter's descent came
on the heels of this mudflow

that suffocated our barnyard
with rowdy epithets and bellows

of mutilated senators
reeling beneath a babble storm

In the landslide that followed
despair arrived on ravens' wings

A tirade of fractious condensations
language of pirouettes

an amalgam of salacious tidbits spewed
from glib tongues were greedily

swallowed by men of the mines and mills
How could we let the currency of our house

be torched in the glaring calumnies
of strutting cocks O we blundered

like blind birds
through the cornstalks of apathy

scrabbled through the underbrush
on fire with the meaninglessness of words

strung like links in a chain of palindromes
All remedies fragile as hope

Baked In

Water roils from one paddle to another
on the waterwheel, spilling
from blade to blade 'till power thrums
in the millhouse, vibrates in the wheel's hub
as it grinds wheat to flour, filling the granary.

We are complicit in the loaves of bread
we bake, the pastries of despair we make,
marzipan and cardamom to camouflage
the mildew in our flour. Raw dough that holds
the power to prove we can rise or fall.

Elites inside white picket fences can enjoy
the whorled beauty of a mille-feuille, or take
leisure time to lick morsels from tines of a fork
full of chocolate pie, while others stagger
beneath the weight of a blackout cake,

rivet their gaze on sugary jewels arrayed
in displays of the pastry shop. Temperature soars
in the oven, brands zebra stripes on damaged goods.
The waterwheel turns as it has for generations,
a juggernaut that drains justice from our lake.

Bitter words are not enough to leaven the dough,
not enough to slather honey on crumpets,
not enough to un-bake what is baked-in, like
bricks set in mortar. No icing can suffice, nor
whipped cream on top. Love's yeast, all you need.

Labor Day 2016

Let the clay, like every other day,
spin on its wheel with its wet imprint

of gray fingers. Let trains rumble through
dusk's blue light, towing Pullman cars

into the night, designed by the man who began
the fight against labor's injurious legacy.

Consider children hobbled at the knee, mere
shadows in dust motes, squeezed to an anemic

marrow, and eyes gone dark as a starless night,
blind as man's unbridled greed. From holy hands

unwound the coolies' toil, torn from
their turmeric and tea, the endless steel

rails snaking across forest and ravine.
For the picket men and the sit-in men

let the rapturous clay spin itself bone-dry—
all that we shape and fire in the kiln

breaks back into sand stripped clean
by nature's tempestuous sea—we cannot

shape time's hydraulic crush nor boast
a rain-bowed glaze that does not fade. Gaze

upon the lumberman's, longshoreman's toil,
their purple bruise of torn sinew and muscle,

my father's face gaunt as the workman he sculpted,
his youth spent as a soldier when world war erupted.

Never forget when the trains rumble through,
the welcome that read, *Arbeit Macht Frei.*

Now return from the picnics and the parades,
work's history eclipsed in a flight of balloons.

Get back to the shapeless lump on the wheel—
Days of our years colored by the pottery we make.

Broken 2017

The road is hard as permafrost
under the bony hand that sweeps

down from the north, rattling
silver dollar leaves gone taut

as snare drums in the marrow chill,
and winter pansies slumped

in their purple tunics, like soldiers
who gave their springs and summers,

now maimed and fallen, who wear
the purple badge on their hearts.

My breath short on the tedious climb
through blackberry and tobacco weeds,

stalks snapped across ditches, groves
of alder and oak, sapwood gripping

down like hope for a thaw in the ice,
a budding of life spun from light

to censure the polling booths of winter.
Sodden leaves mounded up like corpses

in culverts, shrill cry of the eagle
muffled in the forest's deep silence…

Beheaded on TV

Deep set eyes, starkly white
in a hooded face,
betray no shred of empathy
for the man awash in prayer.
No words to mute the sound
that will separate him from his body—

the machete blade's whine cleaving
the air. What's another head
falling to the ground? *These subjects*
may not be appropriate for children.

The image disappears in a storm of static.
Obsessed with the bloodlust of Robespierre,
a scientist theorized that guillotined heads
would continue to have thoughts until
their blood ran out, even as their tongues
lolled in their mouths, in the basket!
Did they think about eating cake?

Goose necks, spouting arteries,
heads on pikes, eyes rolled up in sockets,
my pen trying to light a terrible blaze;
undisciplined syntax spilling like blood
off the page, a bourgeoisie effort
to focus a spotlight on beheading.

On Netflix, the Viking Chieftain shuddered
as he swung his favorite axe, to-and-fro
through the mangled women and children,
licked his lips with their blood.
A gibbous moon bore witness, dropped
a noose around his neck. How long can it go on?

I am numbed by this anesthesia, seduced
by the cruelty of our brothers. Time to flip to 138,
the Travel Channel that highlights a couple
who won the lottery, distraught over a mansion
they bought in paradise, that lacked an infinity pool—
a serious tragedy!

This is how it is after Anne Boleyn.

Amnesia

The seasons follow each other
obediently as sheep, from withered leaf
to nakedness, to budding ingénue.
And we are taught to follow,
as the man in the street comes home
to his shabby flat,
and eats his humble meat. But for
our particular soul, we suffer amnesia.

Mediocrity goads us to walk
"in the footsteps of the greats,"
but the thing that is us, wanders—
travelers lost in a snowstorm, far from the truth
which suffocates in the buried life. Only,
the mediator between the head and the hands,
that is the heart, can unleash the heart.

O' the belligerent babble from despotic mouths,
spewing pixelated hyperbole
into anesthetized minds, seems innocuous
as a campfire's embers before it incinerates
the fawn hidden in the tall grass.

And the spark that triggers Armageddon will come
from men who discovered fire and cherished it,
carried it as an amulet around their necks.
Rusted girders of the A-bomb dome—
a mere 73 years have elapsed, and, we are
on the verge of amnesia.

Lies

Again and again the lies are told,
unfold from tongues emboldened by
wolves of silence that turn cold eyes
on truth that founders, and misery holds.

Lies ride like parasites on lips
that flap until words are unhinged,
and as with fire, truths become singed,
skewed as false premise, fabric ripped.

Our nation teeters on razor's edge
when honest statesmen go unheeded
by cowards who survive, unseated.
Their words shrivel like withered vetch.

My sight is troubled by impotent legions
of men who threaten sky and ocean.
Like spies revealed, their cover is blown,
mans' hubris threatens to end our season.

Bartholdi's Lady in the harbor
weeps for all the huddled masses
that arrived from homes in ashes,
vilified now by lies we abhor.

And who among us would soar like eagles
above the cancerous, toxic emissions,
to counter the lies of a foundering nation,
to suture the wounds of what once was regal?

Inherent in our divine code
truth nestles like an oyster's pearl
accreted in luminous whorls.
Truth's lamp illuminates our road.

Lured

as a honeybee to honeysuckle,
by the basso voice of Leonard Cohen
that shines light through a shuttered house,
by an insatiable appetite
for the medias' bellicose rhetoric—
mind-splitting, repetitious pap spewed
like pablum from an infant's mouth,
the prurient magnetism of voyeurism—
blood sport at a distance, the sin
of pedophilia, fixation on a severed carotid,
or slow bleed of a lacerated liver, or
cataclysmic impact of a hellfire missile
on a remote computer screen, charred
remains of mothers and children,
the macabre silver fuselage of a drone
hovering like a silent mega-wasp.
In love with Maddow, O'Donnell and Hayes,
who amp up the day's catastrophes,
for the liberal intelligentsia in their mansions.

What explains this obsession to rejoice
in the demolition of the other,
hides deep in the brain, like the nugget
in an avocado. And this habituation
to devastation blinds empathy like mud-
spatter on a windshield. Democracy, we,
founder behind an opaque window of hope,
a poisoned whale waiting for the harpoon.

Yet, some, like Cohen sing antidotes:

Dance me to your beauty with a burning violin
Dance me through the panic 'till I'm safely gathered in
Lift me like an olive branch and be my homeward dove
Dance me to the end of love

Capitol Blues

One craves a rare Kobe steak
after months of nothing but smoke,
maybe an artichoke and fat
gutterings from the broiler.

Where have the birds gone?

It's time for the crows to open their beaks
and scream bloody murder.
The moles are cagey though,
and scramble for the exits.

How long 'till the chainsaw falters?

The white dogwood
assaulted by sapsuckers,
locks life in its roots.

What's happened before will happen
again—the bloated behemoth
in his overcoat stuffed with angry cats,
strangles the orchard, douses the sparrows
with petrol, sets fire to the ice.

The hole in the house on the hill
suppurates— an open wound.
Loggerhead turtles joust on the rocks.

But here, we can endure anything,
prepare for earth's orgasmic ripple
to tear down the trellis, flip magnetic north,
and staunch our lacerations
with a patch of purple wisteria.

I Can't Breathe

for George Floyd

Blood runs like water in the gutters,
soaks the earth with its history
of malevolent letting, all the veins
opened now, in its latest iteration,
a collective indignation met with smoke and fire.

So much unleashed from a flexed knee pressed
on the pedestal upon which a man's head rests.
Nights of shattered glass that echo 1938,
of pilferage and pillage, of brandished shields
and batons, flash-bangs and invective, to resurrect

the shining of Lincoln. What would he say
if he could rise, a colossus from his stone throne
and colonnades, to walk the Capital's broad avenues,
war weary in the shadow of history's haze.

He would tell us to remember the blazing heat
of the cotton fields, the overseer's whip cracking
on black skin, the Sycamore's dangling noose,
hobbling, burning and mauling by wild dogs let loose.
Slaughter of fathers and sons, the men and boys
he commanded, who spent their last breath to unlock
our brothers' chains. Surely some justice is at hand,

a time when pigmentation cannot define a man,
when carrying a quart of milk and groceries
down a public street, does not end with the nightmare
of handcuffs, clubs and bullets, vigils and prayer.
In the worst of times, on a rain swept eve, one seeks
a glimmer of light to soften this abject grief.

Hope in a time when blood runs like water in the gutters,
that the four-hundred year old wound is a hole,
through which light pours, to lift the knee
from all who cannot breathe.

Memorial Day 2019

The winds of war still blow fervently
across the plains and rivers of hallowed lands,
and trenches gape like clotted gashes in sand—
Verdun, the Somme and Gallipoli,

where men wore masks to ward off mustard gas.
But it was not enough, this wholesale slaughter
of those who held the torch of freedom, higher.
Came then; Pearl, Midway and Stalingrad.

Up the boot they marched from Anzio,
across the Channel to land at Normandy.
Some drowned like rats to be buried at sea,
others blown up at Gold, Sword and Juno.

Korea, Vietnam and Afghanistan—
the litany never seems to end,
and we with all our wisdom fail to bend
to the truth that only love saves man.

At Pointe du Hoc I stand above the din,
where Rangers spent their lives unflinchingly
in hails of bullets that peppered the sea.
Their cries for freedom echo on the wind.

Storm

Keep going, the wind mutters
through broken limbs of the laurel,
after the blizzard crammed its wolf breath
down our throats, left
husks of despair in the rotunda,
a creeping tarnish on its dome.

Narcissus believes that life's a flash
in the honeysuckle through trysts
of mirrored nights, in thing-a-ma-jigs
that grope before they grab with
greasy jaws. *Keep going*, sings the wind
in bankrupt monotones—*I'll blow down*

your house! Senators siphon off everyone
else, even light from distant nebulas
shaft the scummy air. But you, my friend,
are a case in point—a vicious voice that raves
on rivers of spittle, flips lies like flapjacks
that plummet all the injurious way down

from your tawdry towers of calumny, deaf
to the tonsillar vibrations of a million
mouths, wide open across the great divide.
Nighthawks twitter on branches brimming
with black camellias, oblivious to the carnage.
Few will remember what has been said.

Marjorie Stoneman Douglas

Even as some children ate bananas,
some struggled through algebraic equations,
while others played their last notes in the band.
Always the roll of the dice—
who goes left and who goes right
into a hailstorm from maniacal hands.

We make love and omelets,
are lifted up by sonatas,
kiss our children, goodbye, onto the yellow bus.
Puttering about in blind trust
until some stranger's voice
brings the stage set crashing down.

The lucky ones who wend their way
through life's gauntlet, to walk
beneath spring's cherry blossoms,
can never heal, as long as lunacy stalks our days.

Rushmore, July Fourth, 2020

Where giants enshrined for all time on their thrones,
watch in mute dismay those who mock the forests
where dead men lay, who once hunted and fished beneath
these rocks, see now an emperor of little worth, confabulate,
make promises and oaths, smirk as he throws incendiary
grenades to light the forests on fire as fireworks may.
Such cruelty as can snap a black man's neck troubles him
not, nor can he feel the grief of children stripped away
from their roots, but swoons to all his vassals' fealty.

Surely redemption must come soon, before the bedrock
of our republic crumbles, this nation butchered into chunks
of raw emotion, and Lady Liberty falls from her pedestal.
Hardly is one murder done, then another troubles our vision,
while citizens rampage through the concrete and steel jungles
of our dominion. And circling high above, the red-capped
vultures wait for dreams the founding fathers had, to fall away;
the notion of an equal playing field, ephemeral as fog
the cynics say. Our apathy complicit every day we watch
the snake oil salesman play dice with covenants and laws
that guide our lives. Dark falls, pinwheels sizzle overhead.
Souza marches echo off canyon walls, while killer jets
like hornets tango through the clouds, swifter than wind.

A paradox, this land, home of the brave and the free, where
Sioux women and children were massacred in droves
and buried at Wounded Knee. Their heroes, Sitting Bull
and Crazy Horse knew they must defend their ancestral lands,
as we came to know this sacrifice in World War II. Imperfect men,
the presidents' stolid gaze from their citadel pierces the night, awash
in lights. They seem vexed they were carved with dynamite,
by a sculptor* who eschewed brown skin and black,
as does this rough beast on the podium, so obsessed with reflection
in the pond, he cannot see how inexorably the union suffocates
beneath his tarnish like a knee on the neck. And we, the people,
in all our incarnations, must seize this hour come round, to shine.
Darkness falls, as it has, over centuries of battlegrounds,
leaving Dakota's sky laced with smoke.

*Gutzon Borglum

Corgi Congress

Beyond the blowing seagrass atop the dunes,
the beach seethes with a congress of Corgis,
a blur of tricolor and black and tan fur,
skittering about in their dwarfy dog way
on stubby legs, some leashed, others splashing
through tide pools, bickering and nipping,
trying to herd seagulls like sheep.

Ear-splitting yips assault the senses, indignant
owners like senators, step over small piles of shit,
accuse other dogs of felonies. One bitch,
named, Margot Rose, wears a star-spangled vest
and tows a helium filled balloon behind her
to advertise a rally for aspiring newbies.
Sweating mothers huddle in makeshift tents,
brag about pedigrees, and tell tall tales about
woodland fairies that rode Corgis into battle.

No tolerance for any dog but purebred
as Elizabeth II, here, all others exiled
to the pound. By late afternoon,
this congress is baked, wagging tongues loll,
beer coolers are emptied and bonfires lit
for S'mores to appease unruly children.

One is struck by the capriciousness of it all,
incontinent barking, a silent acquiescence
to utter chaos, the phenotypic similarities
between animals and owners, bloated braggadocio,
and who, exactly controls the end of the leash.
By starlight, the tide erases all but a few paw prints.

Election 2020

An incessant ringing of chimes
as autumn sweeps summer's festering bounty,
and the honks of geese, loud, thumping wings
glide into our meadow for a fallen apple feast.

They do not know of ballot boxes
or man's petty bickering but follow
their own compass, as a vessel on auto-pilot,
over muzzle-flash, mountains and corn fields.

They do what is right for their kind;
stay together for life, lay eggs in the spring,
nurture goslings. They are peaceful at my table,
waddle softly through the fleshy, red-skinned fruit,
drape wings over each other by the shore,
to settle for the night. At dawn, in a thick fog

I hear their clamor, like children rising from sleep,
see blurred brushstrokes of black and white
as they lift away for southern climes. A "gaggle"
better describes my kind, unkind in their pecking
and plucking like caged chickens, sullied nests,
and cracked eggs. Behold that royal entourage

high in the heavens, while we beat feeble wings,
pollute the airways, and cower behind desperate
migrations, smugly, self-satisfied as we ink out
little boxes on a sheet of contenders, and wait
for frenzied voyeurs of our misappropriations,
the morning after, to say, who will weep, and who
might save for us and them, the water and the sky.

Exeunt

2020 goes out like a rabid dog
flinging flecks of spittle in its wake,
awash in wails of the bereaved
as beloveds suck their last sweet air,
cool in refrigerated vans, in car parks.

Pandemonium reigns in the streets, bloodies
our nightly news while the obese grifter
chops divot after divot on the golf links,
double bogeys every hole he plays, gouges
the fabric of our heritage, exsanguinates
what truth is, in a maelstrom of daily lies.

We rail against the racial hatred
that killed Breonna, the knee on the neck
that suffocated George. Against incarceration
of so many innocent black men. Children
ripped from their mothers' arms as bark
from wood, held in chain-link cages and lost.
But memories are quick to fade.

All fall prey to the celestial court on high
that decrees who shall walk on by, unscathed,
and who shall die. We huddle in our bubbles,
cling like Velcro to our flesh and blood, in terror
each day may be the last, eat and drink like starved
immigrants, place our trust in that flawed product
of our brains; randomized, controlled science.

Light years away, Jupiter holds us in place,
absorbs the blows of meteors headed our way,
and deep below the surface, sea vents spew
their primordial soup; the codes for all life
and death encrypted in their alphabet.

From compassion's bottomless well comes its bride,
empathy, to cushion nature's insufferable blows, to hold.

Nearby in a mother's placid lake, floats
a girl-child waiting to unfurl, to usher in hope's dawn…

Caviar

The bellies they slit open
were big and swollen,
knife blades singing to the dumbstruck air
their ovarian song of blood and salt—

Rohingya

Sun scorched the bamboo groves,
the corrugated roofs, the mayhem
of butterflied carcasses, follicles glistening
like nascent eyes.

Somewhere across the globe,
men in high castles made passionate comments
on genocide, but it was time
for the dazzling Times Square ball to descend,
time to sing the song of roe—

Beluga, Osetra, Sevruga,

time to smear the salty globules
on blinis, with chopped egg and crème fraiche,
to swallow down with vodka.

Deep in the river, the behemoth rattles
its armored scales, settles into the silt
for the long, dark night…

Transition Blues

The day on which the vote is certified,
will burn bright as a bonfire in the dark,
a testament to all of us who tried
to resuscitate this nation's heart.

So breathe easy now and listen to
Caesar's overthrow enshrined in song,
and story that Narcissus never knew;
how obsession with his face sullied the pond.

The criminal in the White House cowers there,
vindictive as shrill filibuster rows.
Hope shimmers like the globe above Times Square,
waiting to fall, and fall it will, somehow.

Our congress cannot sanction regicide,
if Lady Liberty is to abide.

Look!

Here's the thing, if you
will permit me to hitch a ride
on the back of a venerable politician,

and the thing is that these things
are killing us; an army of hornets
with razor-edged mandibles,

a biblical swarm of whirring-winged
locusts that scythe our lives in a moment,
while Jabba the Hutt drives another golf ball

into the rough, and gloats over Solo's demise.
I don't want to die waiting for the Jedi
to return, while green-gowned men & women,

God bless them, shove a tube down my lungs
that froth and overflow like a baking soda
volcano in a high school chemistry lab.

So, here's the thing—there's simply no time
for another round of putting, another lick
of the charlatan's boots by his minions who pander

as the buffoon pomades his comb-over cowlick,
or time for a weekend of tantrums and tweets.
Look! Here's the thing. No need to suffer

Skywalker's fate—we have the candidates
for State. Not too late to fire up the crews,
take to the sky and vanquish these invaders.

Join me in a ticker tape parade to honor
the Stars & Stripes, our founding fathers raised.
Chant, ***You're fired!*** as Jabba the Hutt deflates.

Seascape

Drifting and drifting far from latitudes of kindness,
humanity's flotillas languish in the doldrums of contempt.
Hulls are breached, the drowning search for salvation
desperate as castaways clinging to the Raft of the Medusa.

Partisan bickering breaks the bonds of fealties,
dignity erased as tribes swerve from left to right
and back again-- boats adrift without rudders and anchors.

Civility and empathy opaque as lighthouses in a fog,
spawn wrecks on the shoals, mutiny in the ranks.
Consummate loyalty and purity inflame the great moral divide,
a yawning abyss of bleached coral and thorns,
as contempt's juggernaut lurches through civilization.

If you ask what is broken, they will say, *You*, and you will say,
You. Harsh rhetoric scapegoats the disenfranchised.
Opinions eclipse facts and our tectonic plates quake.
Blood libel rears its ugly head, putrid as Buddleia blossoms,
Migrant blood runs in the streets.

The elite will not ask your names
nor the names of your children nor the "whys" of your beliefs--
nothing to them, but ether in a vacuum. Invective litters language
like plastic detritus in the oceans, consensus founders far
from latitudes of kindness.

And yet, and still,
'though winter's sun casts its harsh light across the waters,
kindness gestates in humanity's heart, waits to be born.

Contempt

lays thick as mustard gas
across our nation's trenches,
sucking oxygen from dialogue,
poisoning the roots of compromise.

We have tasted the harvest
of worthlessness, beyond consideration,
less than vermin, choked on the ashes
that blanketed cities and forests,
blinded our eyes, plugged our ears
to the rumbling passage of cattle cars
transporting the despised. Years

have passed since then, yet some
threaten to incinerate again. Rise up
young men and women of honor! Engage
this insanity with passion! Negotiation
is handcuffed by vendors of contempt,
deep lacerations inflicted
on the messengers of truth. No light
shines through the wounds. Truth

is anathema to those who pillage
the palace of justice, and spew vitriol
like agent Orange, exfoliating
our legacy of equality. Contempt

drives its juggernaut through discourse,
flaying kindness like skin to the bone,
murders its sibling, adoration, blind
to love's potential that withers
in a congressional dust bowl, littered
with parched psyches. And when we stare
into our sisters' & brothers' souls, close
as we come through the eyes, and see nothing,

then we are nothing, barren as the space rocks
that hurtle toward our earth, Someone said,
you must love your enemies--that is
our only hope for salvation, even when
creation's debris is on a collision course.

On a Perspective of Things

Everything hinges on belief in the invisible.
Faith follows from this. The suspension of belief
may result in obsession with only the shining surface,
and skew one's life in the mode of shallow thinking.

When the moon obscures the sun, the lovely corona
of rays that escape around the edges, that slight bend
of light proved one man's vision of time and space.

Curiosity for the hidden may seem trivial compared
to the mouth-feel of caramel chocolate, or milk
of the galaxy spread across a darkened sky. Granted,
those modest pleasures are gifts given through tongue
and eye, a foil for what lives deeper inside, if one has
temerity to gaze through a magnifying lens.

Lucretius, a visionary of audacious courage, mocked
by pagan Rome, surmised long before quantum theory,
we came from particles spawned in a time of chaos,
free will depends on the capricious swerve of atoms,
the body, the vessel that holds mind and spirit.

I am riveted by the beautiful mystery, as he was,
even as I struggle with God.

From my home, I can hear shore birds singing
from their nests on the beach, invisible waves that spiral
into my ears. And, intricate spider webs studded
with jeweled raindrops, lure winged travelers.

Most rapturous of perfections is the jiggle of atoms
through the brain, to summon your mind like a monarch,
and command your thoughts,

to secretly lift the veils.

Why

Throughout life we ask the question, why?—
a 3 letter word that clamors in vain.

Consider the pictorial Y:
a trifecta, dowsing wand,
tripod of diverging roads.

Why, the sudden rush from a warm lake
into a delivery room's harsh light
that blinds the first opening of our eyes,
why the sweet, frothy taste of a mother's milk,
soon, taken away, that will drive our appetites
for the remainder of our days. The incessant
whys of children who wield it like a whip—

they will ask us after the swaddle, why
the dog howls, why the boy next door steals
their fire truck, why their sister pushes them
underwater in the bath, why they suddenly
sprout hair in private places—their faces
becoming rough as sandpaper,
why they feel something stir in the presence
of budding breasts at school. Wise men

tell us to never ask, why? instead, to substitute,
how? To detour from philosophical inquiry,
down mechanistic avenues that end in cul-de-sacs.
Still later will come the whys
of good and evil, avarice and philanthropy,
fidelity and infidelity, and so forth and so on...

In the onslaught of years, there will be;
the why, me? or the why not, me? as we watch
beloveds fall like tree limbs in a storm,
our own limbs and body parts succumbing
to the creep of rust, our stories eroded
by the frost of memory loss.

A rabbi who emerged from the death camps, counseled,
if a man has the why to live for, he can bear almost any, how.

The Himalayan blue poppy did not bloom this summer,
despite enriched loam, food and water. Why?

In our senium we plan for the future; annuities,
long term care, cremation or casket, not knowing
how much time is left, what compassion might soften
our departure, whether we will see our beloveds again,
whether faith makes a difference.

Why, all of this, haunts us to the very end,
but I like to imagine a palace of spirits on the other side,
exorcised of all their whys,
swooning in a meadow of blue poppies.

Ukraine

You would not know
on this pristine spring morning
with trees pushing buds into the day,
and Daphne enveloping the porch
in its delicate fragrance, that an ocean away,

Russia's mad monk* has dropped
the first three letters of his name,
to return in a bloody resurrection
of unbridled savagery and slaughter.
Unanswered, that is murder condoned.

We huddle in our opulent dwellings
waiting for fission's flash,
the mushroom cloud that will signal
our end, while our politicians commit the sin
of omission, hurling epithets and accusations
of cowardice, aghast at inflated gas prices.
Horrific, newscasts of women and children
cringing in subway bomb shelters, trapped
in a crush of immigrants at borders.

We have not known the anguish
of children's blood running in the streets,
the hunger, the hopelessness, rubble piled high
in our cities, the scream of rockets leveling
bedrooms and kitchens. These people--
they look, are just like us!

Crude oil runs in the mad man's veins,
as the smirk on his weasel-eyed face
mocks the world on a deadly razor's edge.
One man stands strong against the Philistines;
a descendent of David ready to die
for his nation's freedom.

You would not know any of this
an ocean away on this spring day when
renewal is in the air. Yet I walk with a shroud
of futility and impotence draped over my head,
rage I do not want to infect my soul. Will we
stand by and marvel at the rebirth of flowers?

*Rasputin

Something Beyond

What if mind overflows body
the way nectar spills through the eye
of the coconut's husk, to nestle then
beside other minds or departed souls,
and what if the bridegroom
we call brain is magnanimous
in granting freedom to his bride—
an audacious act, a philanthropic
tour-de-force of release.

Will she wander then as a dragonfly
through the calla lilies or be spun
like droplets from the fins of flying fish?
Or drift blindly as a bat through the ether,
echo-locating a lost love hidden
in the fabric of what the living cannot see,
or will she come to rest on a pillow of clouds?

All this is to say she will leave
that rotunda of sutured bones, empty
as the birth canal she once navigated,
and isn't this what we hope for
in our terminal days—something beyond
the compost heap and searing flames
that await. Even bible burning zealots
turn like sycophants to faith as they draw
their last breath—a bridge to span the loss
of a life too glorious to lose.

Eggs

Anger boils up and risks the egg-
shell will crack and sacrifice its yolk,
congealing white into water that roils
without finesse or urge to quell a yell.

Ego driven we fail to stop and listen
for signals that ring like distant chimes,
the crime a throwback to ancestral brains,
when provocation provokes castigation.

And rhetoric that sizzles like hot coals,
once extolled words like blossoms on a tree,
is doomed to ash within the fire pit,
drifts silently as snow into a hole.

One holds the essence of a soul long known,
more gently than the most fragile of things—
at least one should, for all the grace it holds,
ephemeral as spring's dragonfly wings.

Eggs that are left to simmer in the pot,
softly bump against one another,
without breakage or capitulation.
Hard boiled is served impulsively by a lover.

When given time, shell from membrane peels
like rosy skin from a ripened peach.
To swallow pride means harsh words are forgiven,
leaving each yolk within a glistening sheath.

Blank Canvas

When I cannot remember the taste
of my first Orange Julep,

the tingle of a snowflake
on the tip of my tongue,

rapturous exhaustion as I crawled
over the summit of Kilimanjaro,

the first kiss of my beloved
and faces of my children,

then I shall be an orphaned
animal of the moment—

the impasto of my life
with its vibrant colors, stripped

to a blank canvas of anonymity,
open to a splatter of hailstones

that spark raw nerve endings,
and shatter against

the bolted doors of memory,
storage denied or entry to hold

the pots, pans and bric-a-brac left inside.
An ahistorical man, flapping

like shredded muslin in the wind,
incontinent of laughter and tears,

soul parted from its cerebral moorings,
bobbing like an oceanic sunfish in the surf.

What falls away, some say, is the angst
that propels one through "the roaring forties",

hull stripped of its varnish, down
to the grain of its wood, without memory

of the tree where it took root. A desolate
existential state of mind, most men eschew.
And when you gaze into the eyes
of a woman you knew, the same one

who became your anthem for 50 years,
and cannot recall her name, the canvas

is drowned in tears. But deep within
this atrocious erasure, a faint imprint,

albeit faded as a lithograph in sunlight,
still resides—

of another woman who hums like a bee
deep within a flower, who spooned,

on the day you arrived on earth,
your first taste of honey.

Kite

A dragon kite, silver tail snapping
in the jetstream high above Haystack Rock,
free, yet tethered to a man on the beach,
as when, one goes deep into a dream
of flight through a bedroom window,
to soar over mountains and oceans, unchained
from gravity, 'till a puff of wind spirals the kite
in a dive, and the mind stalls in awakening,
reeled back into containment, to the bedspread
and sheets tucked tight, dark corners of 4 walls,
the dragon's fiery breath extinguished
as it plummets into the sand, as when
freedom's illusion sends youth aloft before
the body shivers in the season's cold draught,
and the kite is wound in, hung on its hook
in a dusty basement waiting to fly again, saying
a dragon hides within every man who yearns
to float above and beyond the rills in the sand,
above a squadron of pelicans hugging the cliffs.
So free, so high, that the Rock below is seen
as a dot. So high, so free, that the word freedom
becomes its own mortician.

The Flow of Being

Late afternoon at summer's end,
I stare at the smooth edge of falling water
as it cascades over the rock's rim,
and then, in mercurial strands of the fall,
I see my life pulled to its rhythmic surge,
harmonic meanders. The currents we ride,
our call to endure, launched into the fray.
Turbulence at the end.

The ant marches, the feline stalks, and we
fall with the water, engulfed by its wetness,
intricacy of its shape-shifting molecules,
all born of the same flow towards the vortex.

Counting backwards, I can hear
the individual voices of tiny droplets
as they burble and ricochet off stones,
then hum as one in a Buddhist chant;
a sonorous sound I recall, trembling
on a ledge behind a waterfall, pluck
that flung me into the maelstrom.

Never doubt the plunge will come,
even when your breath is in synchrony
with the chorus of falling water,
that is life itself, even as you drift
downstream, praying for the man
in a barrel, who plummets into the abyss.

Late afternoon, in darkening light, faith is
the lifeboat we cling to, when falling water
becomes too cruel to bear.

The Tyranny Of

the unchosen
remembers a nascent peach

shunned for the rosy one
hanging within reach

Its velvet skin
and infused honeyed flesh

yields a pit hard and pocked
as the aftermath

of a life unlived
one shocked awake

by the tyranny
of the unchosen

that turns its gaze
homeward and again

to symphonies
thundering in the wind

must now be rendered mute
to bring an end

to cravings
for gifted men's pursuits

the intangible sweetness
of unripened fruit

And as the plovers sing
to celebrate nightfall

embrace the music that holds
each life as a bride

Hope

Try to cherish hope in this life—
steadfast as mothers who breast-feed infants
through famines and wars.

Overhead, autumn storms shear leaves
from boughs, a tornado of red and rust—
fallen apples squandered like trust.

Hold on to hope in this life—
by the brink we pray for tolerance,
men pulled from collapsed mines,

the young woman, shot in the face,
who spreads love around the world. Families
pushed through hell's gates, never seen again.

For the budding of azaleas that carpet
a mountainside, the long upstream journey
from ocean to spawning pool.

Try to nourish hope in this life—
Remember lace curtains fluttering
over lovers asleep in a white cave at Santorini,

the vineyards of St. Emilion—
the vintner's lavender-stained lips. Agates
glinting like moon-glow, hidden on a beach.

Even as the earth shakes, a blue feather
falls from a crested bird, corkscrewing in the wind.
Even as great fires stain the sunrise, crimson.

Subtraction

You must learn to love subtraction;
that tiny dash (-) that commands to take away,
as when the Maraschino cherry on top
of an ice-cream sundae is suddenly popped
into your five year old's mouth, or erasure of
a magnificent sand Mandala, or a snowfall
that covers the paw prints of a winter hare,
or the bones of Australopithecus once clad in flesh.

Revel in subtraction as life's top heavy loads
are unpacked; the minuend minus the subtrahend
(look them up dear reader) gives you the difference,
as when rocks are taken out of a backpack leaving
that exquisite oxygen to hoist you over the mountain.
It's all about mathematics, isn't it? And the beauty is,
one can never achieve absolute zero so total loss
is off the table. What I'm trying to say is that the river

emancipates itself from the land in increments through
alpine brooks, canyons and meadows, spillways
and reservoirs to return to its mother as we are subtracted
back into the earth, as one of us bound by soul to the other
must fall in life's maelstrom, leaving the other until
we are added back somewhere in the cosmos, the echoes
of our passage held in the memories of our children.

You must learn to love subtraction even when brain's
vast forest of neurons is hushed by the deep silence of snow.

Reunion

We have not seen each other for 50 years.
What falls away is terrible—
the hair, the skin, flat bellies, supple limbs,
here, in the dank and hallowed halls of old McGill.
James McGill, James McGill, fitfully he slumbers there
in his Scottish underwear, he's our father,
O, yes, rather, James McGill.

Yet, bright lights flicker in the eyes
of Honey, Bob, Winifred and Roopnarin,
Winifred's guffaws still crescendo like a barking walrus,
Roopnarin's evangelical expostulations
rising to an hysterical pitch about the coming of WWIII,
and, *my friends, what are we going to do about it?*

Bob, the academic regales us with memories
of our first histology lab, when we placed a slice
of salami under the microscope, and, OMG,
saw muscle, bone, blood and ground up teeth
in the viewfinder—shades of Upton Sinclair's, The Jungle.

The anatomy hall is unchanged, its pungency of formalin,
slabs with shrouded "John Doe" corpses (plenty of those
to harvest from a Montreal winter). Here, we walked
in the footsteps of Osler, unzipped chests and abdomens,
guided by Professor Banfill who dissected the bodies
of soldiers in the rice paddies of a Japanese POW camp
to reveal the secrets of human machinery—
the heart ensconced in its castle like a king, intestines coiled
like an anaconda in the jungle—knowledge distilled
50 years later, down to the essence of our fabric,
yet elusive as the mystery of consciousness.

44

Farewell dinner is a formal affair,
spouses in gowns, men fidgeting with Windsor knots,
the few women in the class like royalty on parade.
Anecdotes evoke laughter and tears, especially
when names of deceased colleagues are read,
and suddenly, a voice in the back of the ballroom
booms out, *I'm not dead!* Memories of this student
flood back; truant, brash, me holding on for dear life
on the back seat of his 750 Norton, blazing at 70 mph
down Sherbrooke St., permanently quashing my desire,
not-with-standing orthopedic wards, to ever engage
a motorcycle again. Another colleague reminds us
of our Scottish parasitology professor who provoked
a psychosis in one student who obsessed that the giant
fish tapeworm, Dibothryocephalus Latum had crawled
out of his rear end, necessitating the use of Thorazine.

As for me, I missed Woodstock, my head buried in
Harrison's textbook of medicine, listened to too much
Gordon Lightfoot, and bartended at my fraternity.
On weekends, doted on by my first love who knew
only how to cook spaghetti. The rest of the time,
peanut butter and jelly. Here now, with the love of my life
for 49 years. Then, the clock turns late, and who can say
how those four years, so many years ago, sculpted my clay,
how we labored as one to learn the healing arts,
and wear the mantle of Hippocrates. At evening's end,

one-by-one, the doctors slip away into a rainy night,
and I know I have closed this circle of my life,
and shall not pass this way again.

Blood

flows, driven as lava through the body's
canyons and grottos, bringing its bouquet
of sugar and oxygen to our hungry outposts.

An illusion of homogeneous red, it conceals
an army of warriors and generals,
hell-bent on warding off intruders from outside.

Metallic to the tongue, sticky as syrup
between the fingers, blood is champagne
for the Masai hunter after a lion kill,

baked into pudding or sausage for its taste.
Great gouts spout from the heart
when an artery is cut or a bubble breaks

in the brain or gut—a deadly, torrential gush.
So hidden, only a razor nick will tell,
something unbidden lurks skin deep.

Once, I spilled blood from a deep cut, feared
that it would never stop, that I might not clot,
but like the hemophiliac's lot, bleed out

and look like corpses in the morgue,
with that bluish lake of life's sweet liquor
congealed like gelatin in my flanks and thighs.

This morning, a robin perched in the aspen,
stared askance at me through a snow shower,
and fluffed its crimson breast as if to say,

Live with the thunder of blood in your ears,
you must sing with the blood,
you must sing with the blood!

At the Psychiatrist's Office

upscale décor seeks to calm
— low hiss of the HVAC,
baby-blue ribbed upholstery,
photo-shopped urban skylines,
pine tree reflections on Spirit Lake,
pink neon signs at the fish market
and scattered aboriginal paintings —

emotions scudding like storm clouds,
palpable as humidity, some volatile
as wildebeests driven to the cliff's edge,
others slumped in their chairs like spent
fish at the end of the line, yet others
vibrating in Brownian motion,
on the verge of flying apart. Thumbing

through Time Magazine, I read an article
on Lil Nas X, how this black rapper
dressed in a red cowboy suit, beat all
records with his song, "Old Town Road."
What is it that propels some of us
to a rapturous orbit, while others drown?

Then the nurse beckons from the door,
the bespectacled professor of interior design
cracks his knuckles, unwraps a stale mint,
and bandies about defenses—
sublimation, projective identification
and reaction formation—
how my psyche was sculpted to fit
my father's shape and glaze like clay
on the potter's wheel—
what to do about that? Obsessively
labor driven, ready to bolt for the exit
like panic in a theater when emotions
become combustible.

Weeping in an adjacent room,
a few gut-shredding shrieks,
then silence muffled as a blocked
eardrum. The reassuring hiss
of the HVAC.

Your time is up, the psychiatrist says,
gesturing at a cuckoo clock as he jots
prescriptions for a potpourri
of serotonin enhancers, anxiolytics,
and atypical synaptic cuddling drugs,
he hopes will keep the emotions at bay.
How about psilocybin? I ask,
chiding him for his lip-smacking
and crackling of the candy wrapper.
I tell him it was deeply offensive, as is
his policy of mandatory payment, even
in the event of a snowstorm.
Unruffled, he smiles. Says we can deal
with my anger issues, next session.

In the waiting room, mind-addled patients
huddle like stalled cars. Outside
the traffic swells. I'm going home
to listen to 12 men and women debate
the survival of democracy in the year, 2020.

The herbaceous aroma of mint has left
a bad taste in my mouth. Nausea.
Thunder heads roll in from the west.

The Drowning Pool

How marvelous,
brain chats with every corner of itself,
a garrulous convention of rationality,
frontal to occipital pole and ricochet back,
and then, across the mighty bridge
that anchors music to math.

How splendid,
encoded blips traverse tiny filaments
that flash like neon detectives as they pass,
sifting the contents of our thoughts.

How brutal, when the firewall is breached
by an infusion of Propofol,
anesthetizing the power grid—I recall

a red wave, that spread its oil slick
across my mind as I lay beneath the sheets,
a distant light that winked green
like a freighter's lamp through an opaque fog.

The thud of the shock wave machine
exploding my kidney stone to bits and shards.

I came up gasping, a man from the drowning pool—
the circuits came back online, a bit at a time,
and you materialized out of the gray,
extracted a promise to drink 60 ounces of water
spiked with lemon juice, every day.

I wondered when the agony would spear me
in the flank again, whether, next time the red light
would turn dazzling white,
and all that cross-talk would forever fade
from the chat room in my brain.

How demoralizing
there is nothing to do but embrace the fear
like a terrycloth bathrobe you slip into at night,
the terror that treads water deep in the brain,
like a carp at the bottom of a pond,
waiting for a predator to strike.

Homage to the Heart

Marvelous muscle,
you welcome flotillas
of corpuscles from distant estuaries
into your cavernous chambers,
provision them, launch them
like small boats past gilded gates,
through serpentine waterways,
to distant corners of the realm.

Marvelous muscle,
you do this without syncopation
or delay, resonant as a bass drum,
driven by the demands of every county
in the kingdom, more punctual than
a harbor buoy chiming on the minute.
Through sluiceways the small boats
glide to unload their sweet cargoes.

Marvelous muscle, longevity can
burn a hole through your smooth layer,
knock you off rhythm, wrestle your vessel
to the ground. Then it's crash cart & shocks,
massage & prayer to rekindle your signature.
So many songs extol your name,
with adjectives like throb and broken,
refrains that make a sentient man weep.

Last night as I was sleeping, you warmed me
as does a hearth, gently pulsatile in the cage
of my chest, and I knew you would keep beating
even when my skin and bones had melted away.

Inviolable

We know nothing of the secret life of brain,
even as it propels ideas onto this page,

only what essence evaporates when the nectar
of blood is blocked, or parts are excised

and discarded. If we could hike its ruts and ridges,
rappel down serpiginous arteries and veins,

nothing more would we know of the 3 pound
melon floating serenely in its sterile sea.

Cut it, magnify it—the mystery deepens,
as when a fox eludes the hounds. Shock it

to elicit a twitch, lobotomize, sever
its callosal bridge. Isolated from its five senses

brain withers like corn stalks in a drought.
At autopsy, this vibrant, pulsatile organ

wears death's gray cloak. Listen to the pathologist
pontificate, measure and weigh, pluck out a tumor

that rendered this human unable to recognize
his mother's face. There's simply no way

to interrogate what cannot be seen from inside
brain's domain—no way to take a head and spin it

in a centrifuge, hoping to float nubbins of what
makes it tick. Appreciate the cortical mantle

snug as the polar ice-cap, that presses the brake pedal
to control baboon impulses waiting like lava

to overflow. At war, clad in chameleon's skin, brain
barters virtue, enables men to batter, shatter, impale

without a shudder. Where will you take us
eons from now? Will our urges be purged or must we

remain cunning as crows? We revel in high tech's
genetic code, but the secrets of cerebral splendor

stay locked in time's strongbox, inviolable
and light years remote. Everything we are, the skull

contains—forests and oceans of love and hate,
the quest to delve beyond what is said, dreams to fly

to another place. Brain, teach us to love our unlovable
selves flawed as gemstones forged in rock, forgive

the carnival masks we wear that hold our worst
nightmares of stick men, at bay. By all means,

connect the dots, probe for the seeds, chemokines,
and stars hidden in this infinite garden. Ephemera

become more opaque as answers disappear into
questions, and questions erupt

in a geyser of laughter—something cosmic
that chains us to the knowable place.

To Our Knees

Death comes skittering
like sand grains whipped across a desert,
culls the elderly like a grove of old growth timber.
Wails of the broken and bereaved
darken the moon's sickle poised in the sky.

Branches torn from humanity's tree,
humanity brought to its knees.

Nature's reaper scythes a swath
across the continents, herds us
into burrows like timid animals.
Who shall live and who shall die?
Not I, clamors my voice of denial.

Easy to marginalize death at a distance,
hard when you feel the icy grasp
of its talons closed around you,
as you gather your flesh and blood,
and hold them tight to your chest.
Who will sing lullabies to the children?

Proclamations come down
like the ten commandments from Sinai,
while the buffoon and his entourage
offer golden calf sacrifices.
Other prophets promise protease
and polymerase panaceas, exponential
curve bending to placate the masses.
Charlatans proffer the herb garden for big bucks.
Fat cats barricade themselves on secluded islands
behind stacks of toilet paper, quaff fine wines
and eat chateaubriand.

Containment, like a leaking vein, bleeds
into mitigation. No end in sight holds out
no respite, as microscopic IEDs seed
their relentless rampage. Helical codes
hatch replicas that commandeer our factories,
efficiently as the assembly line in Metropolis.

Hope grips down, bird in the soul,
and sweetest-in the gale-is heard.*

                              *Dickinson

Quarantined

No Mongol hordes with flashing swords
to slash and burn our tender flesh,
or typhus-ridden immigrants huddled
at our nation's door. Who would have thought
these tiny specks invisible to the naked eye,
crowned by a myriad of spikes
and coronas of hidden suns,
a curse from Wuhan's native bats
could invade men's precious lungs.

We cower in our domiciles
like a clan of Meerkats,
not knowing if, or how, or when
the beast like Grendel* will descend
to spark a fire in our chests
until we suffocate and drown.
And so, we tremble in our lairs
like the famine people of Grosse Ile,
Ellis Island's refugees, and Japanese
families interned in camps,
children caged on our borders.

Dread is our justification for isolation,
yet, most severely damaging is quarantine
of the soul, barricaded behind fears
of contagion and otherness; a firewall
that cannot let empathy shine through.

You and I, we clutch our goods, and rail
against being shut in—
no blueberries or Greek yogurt, outings for
Thai food, or beach vacations in the sun.
It's everywhere, this invasion, response must be
draconian. Shortness of breath, fever and cough
threatens like Damocle's sword. Our children

tabulate the 'stats' and count the obituaries,
but you and I, *we're old,* we say. *Let's walk*
the road and listen to birds, watch saplings grow
from aged stumps. Night falls to showcase the stars,
then we climb the stairs to bed, your head
nestled against my chest, and we prepare for
a sunrise that may never come. The virus spreads
without malice, like pollen blown across the earth…

*Beowolf

Easter Sunday 2020

The invaders trickle
like seepage through cracks in a dam,
rivulets, then rivers pour through,
drag us underwater.

No one is immune
to this onslaught that darkens our horizon,
the invisible beasts that dangle
spiked heels and chains over the gauntlet
we must run, our infected dead stacked
like cordwood at the bottom of the canyon.

They gloat joyously as executioners
when our beloveds tethered to machines,
plead for a pristine aliquot of air, in sync
with the red diaphragms that cycle up
and down like bellows. They sing lustily

when the lung's last air sacs collapse,
and you gaze up at their impassive faces
perched like vultures above the ravine,
your vision fueled by flickering neurons
snuffed like a candle's flame.

Saviors swaddled like mummies
in green gowns and face masks
hold our suffocation with gloved hands,
'till the machines are silenced.

And, on this Easter Sunday,
we are left with Andrea Bocelli soaring
on the high notes of Panis Angelicus,
in the vacant Duomo of Milan, the buildings
laved in sunlight, the streets, a desert island.
The Bread of Angels fed to us like manna,
a grace that lifts our hearts beyond despair.

Masking

The men in white coats say,
a mask will save your life,
you must keep your distance
and shun indoor crowds.

So many disguises to hide
the identity of thieves,
or masquerade masks worn
by guests at a Venetian ball,

a raccoon's black-ringed eyes
to aid nocturnal gaze
and tell friend from foe,
the mandrill's face flashing blue & red.

And now, our kind who flaunt
pretty masks with slogans
to ward off spiked intruders that invade
precious air sacs in our lungs.

Yet, these devices, suspended by
elastic bands around the ears,
differ little in their purpose
from the unseen masks that we

all wear—
that vital lie of character
to hold death's executioner
at arm's length

and we, in our Hippocratic guise
as healers, cannot survive
without our ears close to the heartbeat,
or affirmation from an adoring flock.

Strip off your facial covering,
dissolve your papier-mache façade!
Then we can speak truth to our charade,
as when a newborn first sees the light.

Contactless

Ten thousand facial expressions
concealed behind a linen mask,
eyes that say we are terrorized
by these spiked intruders, broken
by prohibition of skin-on-skin,
the delicate brush of lips-on-lips,
and the intimate probe of papillae
on a tongue, the stroke of finger pulps
on neck and thigh. Bumped elbows
permitted, and once a year, aromas
of Daphne and wet woolen mittens.

We endure in our bubbles, delusional
our fortress is impregnable, that we
won't join the spiraling mortality rate
depicted on the Y axis, every night,
that you and I can protect the translucent
air sacs in our chests, escape the hard tube
driven between vocal cords, men dressed
in green scrubs wielding needles & drugs,
or expire in an embrace of tungsten lamps.

We are contactless at the bank, pizza parlor,
hardware store, supermarket where bags
of vegetables, meats and frozen treats
are contactlessly loaded into the car trunk.
We shun any hint of a break in protocol,
in fact, so contactless are we, that we
would gladly prefer an intelligent signal
from deep space, over the critical glance
of a stranger. Contactless is the deep

wound of alienation, a yearning
for what has been stripped from each one
of us; the natural urge to touch, hold tight
as we pass through the hurricane's eye.

Down the Road

You would not know the global grief,
the haggard faces of families,
fingertips forbidden to touch, splayed
against the windows of contagious wards,
on this spring morning walk. The bright
yellow smiles of Scotch Broom in full bloom,
moth-eaten scaffolds of guttered leaves,
a hummingbird's fluted tongue, blossom deep
in delicate exploration of pistils and stamens;
this yearning for sweetness unmatched in nature.

You would not know how he is stunned
on the home stretch of the journey,
by the apparatus of his body—
solidity of a backbone, the glide of femur
on tibia, fluidity of blood pulsing
through arteries and veins to deliver
what keeps him alive stride after stride,
even in the slow slippage down life's rope,
even in the twilight of his demise.
So, he howls with the dogs on the road.

You would not know on this sunny day,
his face was once smooth as the bark of Arbutus,
that he strode through the wards in a white coat,
collar emblazoned with the twin serpents of Asclepius,
and mocked the face of nature's brass-knuckled fist.
How his brethren in hazmat suits
hold each dying breath to the end. He knows
this culling of the herd locates us in the pantheon
of all the species, no higher or lower,
and constrained by the fragile weave of our flesh.

You could not know the rhythmic sound
a ventilator makes, like the rush of maternal blood
he once heard in utero, or the fragrance of lilacs
he imagines with each rise and fall of his chest, or
the birdsong he hears unveiled deep in the silence.

Art in the Time of Covid

In isolation art endures
a butterfly in its chrysalis
that waits like a conductor
to gift its audience with a kiss

I walked today beside Scotch Broom
singing as a wren flew by
Their yellow smiles lit up my room
said I could paint my notes inside

I do not know this prison guard
who is invisible to me
and keeps me chained inside my yard
stifling my creativity

Words spill from fountains of sadness
like Pollock splashed color on canvas

TWO

Diptych

1.

I was wallowing in the doldrums
and the doldrums wallowed in me
I was riven by driven and driven rivened me
into the blueness of the sea whereupon
my boat heeled over and the sea heeled over
on me I cared nothing for the taste of salt
or the silver fish that salted me
On the way to Arusha I drank cow's blood
and the heifers roared like an engine
while the blood ran out of me
I met Mandela on the summit of Kilimanjaro
and he said I was a black man disguised
in white skin I was black and white
and all Africa ran across my louvered lids
I was there when the ice-cap shrank
like a cold scrotum and a cold scrotum
was more than I could bear Silence rang
its vespers and I was silenced in the vespers
of the blue air I lay down in a jungle of thieves
so thick the thieves lay me down and crowned me
there Nothing I cared that the leopard's spots
had faded and peonies bloomed where the spots
went bare I painted plein air 'til the easel
collapsed on me and there was nothing left
but to swear allegiance to the Legionnaires'
blinding sun endless sand sun eclipsed
by the blinding sand I choked on scanty water
from the oasis to emulsify the mushroom's grit
I was heaved up from the doldrums before
the doldrums could swallow me Soon enough
the lights dimmed and I spat like a camel
on a lightless bridge going nowhere

2.

Life rattled my teeth in the cage
and opened my cage into life's
ocean of strife I was lost as a mariner
at sea forever swamped by absurdity
in a kingdom of incredulity Poseidon
thrust his trident at me and I bartered
with mermaids for amnesty The voice
of the conch sang its dirge of lost souls
for the souls lost in fathoms I dove
off the shores of Wakitobe Gongs rang
in the cupolas that rocked like ducks
in the roiling swells I sought shelter
under a pergola and prayed for salvation
in Hispaniola Drank Pisco sours in Cuzco
Peru at the Quechua Blues Bar Café where
Bob Marley and The Itals came to play
Outside rose the spire of Salkantay where
avacados like pendants hung in arrays and
Inca shamans roamed through the trees
Through the roaring forties I cowered
in the maw of the wind that roared
through me all the way to Iceland's shores
I was pyroclastic and flow in a blast
of tephra and pumice Ate rotted shark
baked in the ground and pink-footed goose
washed down with flagons of Black Death
and Black Death washed me down like so
much salt in the scuppers There was nowhere
else to go on this island bloodthirsty
as Pissarro so I picked up my teeth
which had begun to sprout and put them
back in the cage Began to travel the path
some poet said I should make I was gaveled
by life's gravel and grit but paid the bond
to emerge in the light I howled like a coyote
at night before I sailed my vessel at dawn

After Jack's Heart Attack

he lay on crisp, white sheets, hallucinating
bicycle wheels, how each revolution
must come from the injured sack, fibrillating
behind ramparts of ribs. Care-givers' voices
grew loud, then faded like children's, playing
tag in a forest. Capture the Flag, had been
one of his favorite games. Pablum passed
like prayers between his lips. He thought this was
heavenly and forgot the texture of meat; predatory
instincts edged away to some archetypal niche.

Breathing became sprint— he recalled a cinder track
where lungs quit down the stretch and knees
pounded on like an automaton, as if, they no longer
required the blessed sacrament of air. Toward the end,

doctors spread his chest, glued a patch to the pump,
to revive this dying horse. Wire sutures trussed him
together like a Thanksgiving bird. Wrist and ankle
restraints, he imagined as bracelets suspended by
pulleys from the ceiling. At night, these lifted him
into air where he swam weightlessly, flitted brilliant
as a firefly between hard shafts of surgical steel.
When that battered fist of muscle called heart, finally
ground to a halt, he was soaring through the forest,
bathed in mosaic columns of light,
unaware of the crashcart's shock, listening
to the whole universe call his name.

Hot Tub Man

The man in the hot tub
sits kitty-corner from me,
body shrouded in a towel,
head in a hoody, dropped

like a limp duck on his chest.
Through the steam, his thighs
are pale white as an albino's,
or a man bled out. Malevolence

sends a cold tingle through
my overheated body, jolts
my post-Cartesian consciousness
like a cattle prod. Reality

struggles, a drowning animal
trying to save itself. I know
he is alive when he suddenly
gazes up at the ceiling tiles,

eyes rolled back like white
marbles, the way our ancestors
in volcanic pools must have
looked up at a star-studded sky.

Is he a disciple of Opus Dei, or
incarnation of a modern day
Moloch? Where the eyes feast,
mind lures image like insects

by a Venus flytrap. So how can
we be sure of what is flesh, or
what we choose to call flesh?
The jets hiss like vipers.

In 1970, I wandered through
the contagious wards of a big
city hospital. There were men
like this man, there, slack-jawed

open-mouthed, on the way,
others with tongues lolling from
the corners of their mouths,
who had already passed the gates.
Consciousness hangs by a thin string,
greedy for all the tributaries that feed it,
that make it sing. Tenuous as a kite
held aloft in a breeze. I surface

from this intermission of memory.
Sun streaks through a skylight, sets water
droplets on fire. The man across from me
has vanished. Was he an illusion or some

doppelganger come to humble me? To say
I could not see what was in front of me, or
what will be. The water's tumult fades
into a web of whispered mist.

The End of Jack

does not go gently into that good night,
nor rave or burn at close of day,

but struggles in a stuffy room
and narrow bed—
Jacob wrestling with the angels,

Jack's heart convulsing in a tug-of-war
with his lungs, a seed clinging to its pod
that rattles in the wind.
Death louvers lids over pinpoint pupils,
drains the brain, and smears its waxen make-up
on sunken cheeks, dulls the gloss
of his leonine mane of white hair.

Short days ago, this impresario of Bunuel films,
disciple of Leonard Cohen, Piaf
and Beethoven's quartets, brilliant mathematician,
felt life ebb from his mind and body—
the end of *La Vie en Rose* spent decomposed
in a chair, before the television screen.

If I could ask him now, he would have said,
Non, je ne regrette rien—I regret nothing.

And with life's last sweet breath,
the petite Parisian woman you adored,
just returned from the funeral director, says,
Now, I need to feed the machinery of death.

Rage no more dear friend. You leave indivisible
as the numbers you adored.

Farewell W D Clay

Now, death's mask scrolls across
this dear man's face like some hideous
parasite from the other place. And, breath

a timid animal escaping from the cheeks
that weakly inflate and deflate, straining
to lift his chest, four limbs inert and mummified

beneath the sheets. Still, a beatific smile
plays softly on his lips, and in the final days,
as stoic as a man could be, you thanked life

as does a tree for all its seasons of brilliant color,
aware the sap would sink back to its roots,
and leaves would shrivel and fall.

O' friend you were a mariner who sailed
the roughest seas, painted your heart on canvas
like wind upon a sail and in words

that tacked and reached across the page.
May all pain cease now in the arms
of your beloved mate. O' grace of light

dear man, as your widow lovingly ladles
your ashes with rose petals into the sea,
they glimmer in that shaft of sun,

resplendent as your life, as they slowly sift
beneath the Urchin's hull to the ocean's bed.
Go gently now in the ebb-tide

to heaven's open arms that wait, cherished
by those left bereft in your wake,
faces you will know again beyond the gates.

Cemetery

I pass under a granite arch,
drenched by a light drizzle,
into the home of the dead.

Tombstones as far as the eye can see,
spread across
the manicured hills of Mount Royal.

A treasure hunt for my mother and father
waiting for me,
my cousin who took his life at age 30.

Up and down the coiffed rows,
holding a soggy map, locations smudged
in highlights of yellow and pink.

Their names suddenly luminous
in the trickle of rain down marble,
unbidden throttle in my throat.

Betty, my mother, my queen,
my life-raft through all of childhood's storms,
who opened the doors of possibility,

Reuben, my father, who clothed and fed me,
who taught me what work means, the paths
of Torah, how to blow the shofar.

Uncle Joe who held me on his knee, listening
to the Met Opera broadcasts, aunt Anna, who
taught me to pick my teeth behind a napkin.

Their atoms have joined
Adam's atoms in the cavalcade
of atoms returned to rest.

I plant a kiss on each headstone,
turn to watch beads of water
slip from red Begonias to the earth.

Batman Lego

I am four again, stretched out
on the floor of my grandson's bedroom,
imagination reborn, backache ignored,
the accretions of 75 years stripped away.
Behold Gotham City with searchlights,
skyscrapers and clock tower, all lit up.
Batwing suspended in a blue halo.
Play acting with cudgels, boomerangs
and missiles, awaiting rescue
by a pediatric Batman with flaxen hair,
cloaked in a black cape, hissing,
as he blasts the Joker with twin cannons.
Heath Ledger intrudes on my fantasy
as I attempt to mimic his maniacal laugh.
Batman arrives in the Batmobile with Robin,
to break grandpa out of jail. This drama
ends as suddenly as it began, when
he streaks out of the room to commandeer
Dada's computer and place another Lego set
into his Amazon cart. I am wrecked
on the floor, groaning on all fours.
In the morning a full blown tantrum
when he cannot find his Batman jacket
to wear to pre-school. On the way,
he says to me, *good guys need guns to kill
bad guys.* I tell him about the Lone Ranger
and Tonto chasing bandits. *Hi Yo Silver!*
My daughter, newly pregnant,
raises one eyebrow and shakes her head.

Encounter

The day started with a faun on the road,
spindly-legged with aqueous brown eyes,
mother close by, watching this alien trudge
uphill. I stopped beneath a canopy of trees
through which light poured onto the faun's
dappled coat, white spots ablaze in the wood's
dim glow. And I thought;

I cannot know what the faun sees, as when
a fetus is thrust from its amnios, and gazes
for the first time at a maternal face, the first
glimpse of beauty that will dance with terror
through the arc of its days. Stunned by the moment,

I left my life and knew a divine harmonic,
woven into the fabric of the cosmos.
And I wanted to start over like the faun,
to absorb sights and sounds, smells and touch
baked into life's layer cake.

The distant yelp of a dog broke the spell,
and with a flounce of hindquarters like a coquette,
the deer bounded over an embankment studded
with blackberries, where I could not follow, but
was followed by this splendor to the end of the road.

Looking Back in the Rearview Mirror

through a bramble of "what ifs," and "if onlys",
is futile as self-flagellation for "snap judgements"
and "snappier decisions". For example, sinking
an empty beer can to the bottom of the Apple River
in full view of a hidden, armed Park Ranger—
11 hours in a cold jail cell wearing only a bathing suit,
good friends who bailed me out. Still makes me shiver.
Or when I paraglided on skis, off a glacier, high flying
as an albatross with red wings, aware I could plummet
like a stone, break every bone in my body. What splendor
the sun-split clouds, the rush of air, the shouting wind,
the unblemished rush of it, the laconic descent, squeaky
sound of skis on snow. One less cat in the nine lives.

Dive with me on the reefs of Taveuni, in a cloud
of Anthias like purple raindrops. The sudden appearance
of a Tiger shark 2 feet from my face, a wolfish gaze
that made my blood run cold as reptilian blood. Air blown
from my lungs as I edged away, rising like champagne bubbles
to the surface, to celebrate another escape from the jaws.

The hospital years shaped me as clay on a wheel, pulled me
through the wards of the feverish and dying—
the immigrant with worm cysts in his brain, a man
who spouted blood from broken veins in his esophagus,
an addict who killed my patient by injecting heroin into the IV.
Mea culpa! The woman who delivered a son into her pantyhose
in the back seat of a speeding car! So many souls gone to rest
in the rearview mirror, Christ, why am I still floundering about?
What if I had become a conductor, chosen baton over stethoscope?
Feted on the podium by adoring fans after a muscular performance
of the Brahm's 3rd symphony in classical Toscanini style. How
would that have shaped my life going forward?

To romance. How I made a snap decision cloaked in the ineffable
when I met you—the eyes, the way you carried your lithe body
on the dance floor with an imperceptible coquettish flounce
to the beat of Aquarius, how you perched on my knees underwater
in the green lights of the swimming pool. A fifty year intoxication
anchored in passion and friendship. A brisket smoked to perfection.
Something to savor and enshrine in the stars forever. The grassy patch
at the blind end of the labyrinth that holds this orchard's last aroma.
*Je ne regrette rien.**
I regret nothing in the rearview mirror.

*Edith Piaf

Koons, Poons & Cattelan

Bloodied after 24 hours of broken minds and bodies,
lead poisoned babies with big heads and cigarette burns,
gore rising in my gut and outflow of water from my eyes,
I scribble a bill of lading for the medical chief
in the ivory tower across the street—all he cares about
are labels and numbers—dump my grimy, puke-stained
scrubs in the hamper, put on my raincoat and head for
the mid-town Manhattan subway from Prospect Park,
hoping for something, anything that could elevate my
battered mind. I don't know precisely what I am seeking,
so I wolf a Nathan's hotdog smothered in cheese and chili
from a pushcart vendor in the rain, and stare at smeared,
orange and green stoplight reflections on the wet asphalt.
I chafe at the "Sold Out" signs for a matinee performance
at the Metropolitan Opera—one aria could have lifted me
onto a celestial plane, but wander instead into the MOMA,
up the winding white marble walkway, crowded by NY chic
in stiletto heels, shouldering Prada and Vuitton bags. I admit
I have never understood Pop art, but detour to see Cattelan's
14k. gold toilet, a satirical jab at the affluent who must shit
just like the poor. Surreptitious giggles do little to lighten
my heart as I flee the scene into the next delicacy, Rabbit—
a shiny, stainless steel balloon bunny fabricated by Jeff Koons,
that sold at auction for 91.1 million—a testament to white male
privilege, (fuck like bunnies, make more money, the one with
the most toys wins). I used to assemble bunnies out of red
balloons at birthday parties. A certain desperation gnaws at me,
to find something real, to draw me towards it, to hear the keening
beneath its skin. I disengage from the voyeurs ogling an orange
pubis, a man who glides by like sushi on a conveyor belt, bent
on seeing everything (nothing) before closing. Color sweeps me

into the next room, oblivious to everybody passing through,
a vibration that rivets me to a canvas by Larry Poons, who made
his mark with dots on monotone backdrops, but exploded
in mid-career through concrete walls to lavish tactile pigment
in every shade and nuance of creation. Stunned by his passion
and sheer homage to splendor is as close as I can come by image
to Keats's definition of truth. I want to curl up and sleep beneath
this rapture, breast stroke through its labyrinths and corridors,
baptized by its colors, to awaken to light pouring across its rain-
bowed vista. I lose myself in the warp of hours until a docent
taps me on the shoulder. Back outside, a sleeting rain pulls me
into a vintage cheesecake deli. I watch the work weary go by,

jostle for Yellow Cabs, the sky, a black ribbon woven between
roofs and towers. Then, my train rumbles back to Brooklyn's
contagious hospital, where a mosaic of faltering humanity waits.

Epiphany

for Alisha

Life says, don't expect an epiphany
anytime soon— that sudden scattershot
of dazzling sunspots that lift you above
your gravitational center and float you
like a feather in the breeze. Instead,

focus on the small miracles whispering
around the edges—
brittle leaves underfoot that crackle
like a swarm of grasshoppers scything
through a wheat field, a pygmy frog
frolicking in a rivulet on the road, pine cones
littered in the gutters; summer's last
fertile hurrah, slow motion puckers in puddles
made by raindrops, Puffins nesting high atop
Haystack Rock, the dunes forever shifting.

And you, daughter, on this windblown day,
nestled like a swan before the hearth, you,
holding such wonder within, a perfect harmonic
of your own heartbeat, an anodyne
to the darkness sweeping our world, will bring,
like the roots that grip down to crown their stems
with blossoms—
the longed for epiphany, that is life itself.

Cancer

23½ degrees north of the celestial equator,
the sun finds its northernmost latitude,
bids the flowering trees to give up
their blossoms to the wind, frosting
the meadow like icing on a cake. One arrives

alone in the Tropic of Cancer to read
the report's conclusion that shutters a dream
of unfettered possibility. How did you pick
the lock and creep through the back door
while our party was going on, blight
the Iris blooms and render the aspens silent?

Your greed to dominate and lay waste
to the villages around you, be it or not a fluke
of nature is reprehensible! This is worse than
a stun grenade; being launched by an explosion
into a future of invasion and bone pain. As for
God, as usual, he is nowhere to be seen.

I need to ponder my despair in seclusion, to rock
on the back porch without words, face to face
with myself, and watch a barge on the sound
nudge north with its burden of coal, to accept

I must go with the tides. So many fine years
rife with desire, growing roses for my darling,
so many fine years we listened to the beat
of hummingbird wings, shared in their passionate
courtship dance, were awakened from wild love
by spring timpani played by sapsuckers
on the downspouts--what a fanfare for us!

So let the thunderheads come and the rain thrash
against the windowpanes, let me fall asleep
to the sound of geese in the tall grass, huddling
for night beneath folded wings.

Silent Signals

Tree swallows wheel in unison
high above the Maples
like a flag snapping in the wind,
swift as a bait ball of mackerels
shining underwater. Our instincts

opaque to unspoken signals,
our minds in flight and fight
to control our enigmatic souls
invisibly woven into their matrix
designed for locomotion
or change of vector on a blustery day,

this day when I imagine my family
sky-dancing over a canopy of lace
on the way to refuge under the eaves
of Capistrano—

mother with her heartbroken eyes,
father hollowed out by infirmity,
the others, blurred faces in the mist,
free now as the birds. As I gaze up,

sun kindles the flock that sweeps
like a searchlight across the heavens.
I know they cannot cross over, yet
memories of those sentient beings
pull me up the muddy road,
bear me aloft to a nest in the sky
where the swallows fold their wings.

Murmuration

I catch in mid-morning flight
a burnished black unison of wings,
a seraphim angel guarding God's throne
air brushed across the sky, that pivots
as one through sun-split clouds,
and sweeps smooth into the next angle
against the wind stream on high, wheels
and weaves as one balletic wing through
sizzled air, driven by silent commands.

We are a swarm ourselves, a shape-shifting
harmony that is a state of grace, driven by
inner swirling at the edge of a dusky sub-
conscious, mirrored like birds against the sky.
To be close to the other, but not so close
as to collide. When was cohesion lost?
When we hoarded fire, snapped our teeth
on animal bones, savaged ourselves with
twisted tongues, set a crown upon our brains?

Science opines that every seventh Starling
signals its comrade a time to turn, as when
a platoon on parade abruptly shifts direction.
Thus, the entire flock follows; seven upon
seven upon seven… In this mid-morning
delirium of precision, I stay rooted to earth
gazing up, and exalt every divine thing
I do not believe in. Stay until that dark shadow
no longer shapes my vision.

For the Dearly Departed

The air brisk, the downpour steady
and unrelenting. From the back porch,
the island shrouded in mist, where
I envision the faces of my brothers....

In that feckless bloom of adolescence
we were insouciant as D'Artagnan
and the three musketeers—
on the hockey rink, at the prom, (where
I spilled prime rib juice on my shirt),
in prurient infatuations, and then,
fraternities, and longed for roads to glory.

How often in the fog of becoming men
we were buffeted into the eye of the storm—
Michael to Uganda under the hammered-skull
policies of Idi Amin, Danny to Paris
as a strip club bouncer, Carl and I, to
the overpowering reek of formalin
in the cadaver lab, with scalpels in hand.

Our engines fueled by hope and expectations.

Dear Michael, you took the coward's way
in a field of flowers, and you, Daniel,
overdosed when a money deal went bad, leaving
two sons and a devastated widow. Carl, master
surgeon of joints and bones, a ballooning heart
that pumped an endless stream of love, marooned,
then killed you, flung your sweet wife into madness.

Now, I seek solace in silence,
death's incomparable couch, as I mourn
that ancient wreckage that perpetually washes up
on my shore. A hard rain ends it all.

Introspection

On the way to the Stop sign,
I pass Scotch Broom dessicated
to white ash, a snakeskin flattened
on the asphalt glinting
like a black opal in the sun.

Swallows brush a luminous swath
across a cobalt sky, curtained
by their passage. A bird's lilting trill
high in the trees, recalls our journey
to Desolation Sound, that became our song.

An iridescent blue dragonfly
alights on a leaf--everything lit
on this day of shimmering heat.
This day I march toward
the red & white octagon at the end

of the road, trailing ghosts behind me--
the young men who left the scene early
to curl up in a field of flowers. A small cairn
of white stones that shines with the impermanence
we fervently deny. Last year's pine cones

splinter like bones underfoot. A bronze plaque
with the name Jeffrey Lillybridge, 1981-2000
behind a carved cherub ringed by stones--
cut short in his prime. A game of chicken
on a slick road, or nature's capricious executioner?

What does it mean to stop,
to see with clarity through life's illusion,
through the mirror's silver emulsion? To know
the man I have become. I pause to watch
cars whiz by, listen for whispers in the pines.

Afternoon Practice

Arpeggios float up from the basement
as aromas waft from a bakery, to christen

this rainy afternoon with memories
of a day, forty-five years ago,

when you glided like Aphrodite
down the marble staircase of Clara Madsen Hall

to sit at the Steinway, and bring alive
the Appassionata, for me, an audience

of one. I still envision your fingers
sweeping across the ivory and ebony keys,

precise as a sculptor who lives in the grain
of the wood he shapes, and knows

the history of each ring laid down
by the tree that tells the story of its life.

Your spine straight as a plumb line,
muscles rippling beneath a silk chemise,

slender arms and hands that spanned
the genius of the composer, to coax

each nuance of the hammers and pedals
against strings deep within the larynx

of the piano. One has only to marvel
at the valor of a woman who has carried

this passion within, all the days of her years,
like our children she birthed and shepherded

through a harried life, to resurrect now
the tempi and tempestuous majesty

of these passages. Through repetition comes
cadence—the exuberant flow of the river

in harmony with its banks. I wait for last notes
to fade behind the soft gush of the downspouts.

The Falls

After the river has flowed through meadows
and sun drenched canyons
and after it has witnessed the birth of flowers
and survived lassitude in a drought
after 45 years when I gaze into your eyes
I know we have entered water's quiet eddy
before the falls
I would hold you here forever
turning like two leaves joined at the stem
spinning slowly under the stars
deaf to the whir of turbines
to the din of voices above the dam
and diesel trucks carrying payloads to nowhere
I see only your eyes
before we are swept over the rocky lip
into the plummeting spume
to fall inseparable at equivalent speed
unriven by vortex or time
to sleep at the bottom a painless repose
so hard to let go after a life well loved

Walking with Mozart

Today, I listen to Mozart's 23rd piano concerto
played by the late Vladimir Horowitz,
his power, agility and nuance, coaxing
everything the hammers and strings have to give,
lifting me into another world. Nearby, a rooster
launches into a chorus of cock-a-doodle-dos,
horses whinny behind a hedge, and a small cairn
of white stones by the roadside, flares in the light.

Lightness of being graces the *allegro* movement,
gives lift to my gait, high-stepping as Clydesdales,
then slips into the melancholy of the *adagio*,
hauntingly melodic as his soul. The *allegro assai*
finale, frenetic in its dash to the finish, as if,

he knew the metronome was running down,
hastens my journey home with a wind at my back,
my head on fire with music, astonished that
the human mind could create something so sublime.
The woods silent, notes held like eggs in a nest.

Zoo

The jaguar slinks into tall grasses,
the tapir, swinging a vestigial trunk
to and fro, scurries into its mud hut.
The Komodo dragon hidden from sight,
sunbathes in a private garden.
Only the giraffe sticks its neck out
like a shipyard crane, eager to unload leaves.

Everywhere posters announce a plunging tally
for survivors from the ark. O' white dove,
with the olive branch in your beak, you could not
foretell Noah's legacy. We hide behind masks

of righteous indignation, slogans of passionate
concern about extinction, shrinking habitat,
food chains, poachers and apex predators.

I gaze into the face of an orangutan and feel my own
despondency, severed ties to the forest's stillness,
but I am towed by my grandson along the savannah path
barraged by a litany of gleeful exclamations—
I would swap my eyes for his in an instant, so shining
and drawn by exotic wonders. In the corporate

butterfly garden, Mozart is piped through speakers
while tourists in Mexico trample Monarchs underfoot.
I shall say nothing to the small boy holding my hand,
eating cotton candy, who thinks he has discovered Eden.

There are no fig leaves here as we search for escape
from the zoo of our creation, for hope beyond
our desecration. Who is staring impassively
into our cage? There will be no place to hide

when the lion comes gnashing his teeth…

In Memoriam

for Aria

The way light hones an edge on break of dawn,
a flash of yellow wings comes through the leaves,
coaxes the eye to see or not to see
her essence rising like the mist, lives on

over this meadow sloping to the shore.
She sleeps beneath the old magnolia,
lulled by the chirping of cicadas.
Six years have passed since death locked the door.

What falls away cannot be saved,
as when a child never sees the light,
spilled from its chrysalis before its flight,
and denied this world's sweet air to taste.

We know so little of the journey's end,
fragile as reeds in the wind we bend.

X-mas Heart-string

When the horse could not breathe,
grandfather towed it with the tractor
away from the barn to the creek,
shot it in the head, left her there
for the coyotes and crows, the way
some monks are left for sky burial.

Told his three-year old grandson,
Bonnie had gone to a happy place
where all old creatures go to rest.
When the boy asked if he could visit,
his mother said he would always be
attached by a heart-string he could pull,
to let Bonnie know he remembered her,
the times she carried him on her back.

Later, the boy dreamt he would die,
asked if Dada would come to see him
and Bonnie in that place. His mother,
speechless, felt a great weight crush
her chest, fought back sobs. The boy
waited like the dog waiting to be fed.

When her throat unclenched, she said
he would not die until he was very old,
had many children and grandchildren
of his own, reminded him to pull
on the heart-string whenever he felt sad.

And you, my mother beneath the snow-
laden meadow, can you feel this son pull
on the heart-string stretched so many miles?

Then they sat around the tree adorned
with lights and baubles, and opened gifts.

Digging for Worms

for Aden

The small boy with flaxen curls is knee-deep
in mud, digging for worms, studiously
as a crow fixated on bright, shiny objects,
unafraid as yet, of cryptic, writhing things. He wields

a miniature trowel, squeals with delight
when he unearths the pink, accordioned prize
and scoops it into his hands. *Worm, Doodah* (my nickname)
he utters in newly parsed language, then calls
for more. We hunt in vain beneath a California sun,
until orange stains the horizon. Something primal

stirs in me as we comb through twigs and stones,
between the roots of a dormant blueberry bush—
the love that flows from each cherished moment
with my daughter's son, regrets for all the hours
I have spent divorced from this earth, for the soil
that has never sifted through my fingers, for the time
father plunged my hand into a can of throbbing
night crawlers, fostering fear and shame. Now,

my grandson points to a shallow hole in the ground—
a burial place where he gently sets the worm,
and smooths a layer of dirt like a blanket over its body,
informs me it's time to go, *night, night.*

There is no way to estimate the exuberance of muddy
knees and hands, soaked pants, and a mother's open arms
on this stellar afternoon of afternoons,

to sing in all its glory, an anthem to the worm.

Deep Freeze

The north stiffens,
hurls its fury into the lowlands,

cold and quixotic, hardens
everything it touches.

Ferns, like nuns in white habits,
kneel across the mountainside,

dollar plants drop their coinage
in the freeze, to fracture in muddy ditches.

Throaty voices of remote generators
play the song of our fragile survival.

One holds the silence here
like the lifeless body of a soft animal—

what lingers after the sound barrier
breaks. I walk down the road,

search for nubbins of green
poking up between broken branches.

Past fir trees that palm their burden of snow
like platters. Everything here calls one

to sleep, even the rhythmic whump
of an owl's wingbeats through the woods,

muffled by winter's crystalline flurries.
Our footprints leave bruises in the snow.

Bald Eagle

There's something to envy
about the Bald eagle that waits
patiently, as I cannot wait patiently,
for a silver shadow to glide,
a litany of words to cascade,
beneath the waves onto the page.

Something to learn from the folded wings,
the hooded eyes, the hooked beak,
poised as I cannot be poised. And,
the white headdress catching the light
while I meditate in darkness,
biding my time, as does the raptor
for something to fatten the day.

There's something to envy
about the talons, those scaly, grappling claws
that anchor the bird to the bough,
as I pull anchor, a boat in an ebbing tide.
Then, precision of the dive, talons lowered
like landing gear, to pluck the prize, to dangle
before my eyes, all that has passed me by.

When all I have to lower is the nib of the pen,
with an inglorious push of the thumb,
but it stays retracted, uncertain the runway
will come. There's something to study
of magnificence, but I cannot find words
for the vigil, dive and pluck, that will suffice.

Cloak me eagle, in your pristine crown
and tail feathers, spread a benediction
on the wind, that I might soar with single purpose,
and sing beneath the sun.

Moss

comes out from hiding
like hedgehogs in spring,
when leaves of summer fall.
Drips like candle wax from boughs,
spreads across roof shingles,
and decorates each crevice
between flagstones. Haircap,

Heath Star and Baby Tooth attract
Bushtits and wrens that scatter
like grains of rice tossed at a wedding,
hide like refugees in the moss,
feed on small insects living there.

Moss wanders into deep river valleys,
soothes rocks' sharp edges,
fashions a green pillow for any soul
in need of rest. Why then, do some
label it a pariah, the way they do
to the lowliest of their own,
spray poison 'till it withers?

Three-hundred million years
of adaptation for perfection leaves
one in awe of this survivor, at home
in a metropolis or in the woods.
One like me who is launched
into the world's maelstrom, to run
at breakneck speed, oblivious
to the trajectory of a rolling stone.
And after we are no more, moss
will spread its spores like pollen,
to repossess the bones of our home.

Frog

I spot him after the rain,
in the catchment basin
beneath the downspout,
immobile, the color of moss
and granite. A slow drip

pushes concentric ripples
behind him. I am mesmerized
by his statuesque demeanor,
essential frogishness,
placid patience,
and wonder what lessons
I might take from him,

whether he conceals
a prince inside, waiting
for a princess to sing
on a lily pad in the pond,

if he can teach me to cherish:

the silence of snow falling,

to wait for a slack tide,

the art of the slow breath.

A few days pass, and I observe
the skin of his back, blanched white.
He has died, yet his legs hold their green hue,
as if he clung to the final moment,
to the water that was his life.

And I think he was saying something
about how precious and finite
that thing we die for, is.

Rhapsodic

A shocking spectacle at dawn—

two robins cavorting on the lawn,
wings flailing, flipping upside-down,
mounting from the rear, bright flashes

of crimson breasts—an audacious act
of copulation, a verisimilitude
to expressions of lust in our species.

The female skitters up into the sky,
the male, hard on her tail,
as in an aerial dogfight.

When was it that domination turned
to a feathering of lips on lips? When
the ineffable riveted the gaze of lovers.

Arrogant of me to conclude there was
no pleasure in the robins' tryst—indeed,
how can I know what birds feel?

No matter, the image has stayed with me—
how love grips down in all its forms;
virility, fervor, tenderness

when our bodies are entwined
and the cymbals clang overhead, when
love is enshrined in the dance of spring.

Pine Cones

litter the ditches like tiny armadillos
when spring catapults into summer, when
their pollinated seeds are scattered
by squirrels, extruded by fire, blown by wind.

My season has flown, procreation spent,
each cone a symbol of enlightenment's third eye,
wisdom's gate that has yet to open.
Neruda knew the pine cone's power, traded
a wooly lamb for one, through a hole in a fence,
with a boy he had never seen.

Named for a pebble-sized gland,
the pineal nestles deep in our brain's inner realm,
spreads a soporific potion over sleep and ovulation.

I stoop to pluck one from the dust, marvel
at its armored plates strung in a tight spiral
to its central core, layered as baklava,
its coniferous husk that vibrates like a sparrow
cradled in my palm, the echo of power, spent.

The cones swirl around my boots, are slowly ground
into dust. Somewhere, a new pine tree takes root,
elsewhere a coffin is lowered into the ground,
in the birthing suite, another uterus gives forth.

Un-blind me! Tell me why
the perpetual engine goes 'round.

But the earth remains silent, holding its rhythms.

Come Late Summer 2020

smoke hangs over the coast
like grief shrouds the bereaved,
great fires raging south and east.
Families huddle beside charred bones
of homes, blackened car chassis,
a teddy bear stained with soot.

Annihilation by pandemic or fire
drives the living to cower in bubbles
like Parrotfish do, to ward off sharp-fanged
predators. At summer's wane I trudge
uphill past rust-tipped ferns, spider webs,
shriveled pine cones; procreation's last gasp.

One chases hope this side of the grave
with the naiveté of an addicted gambler
on the precipice—
in the peals of children's laughter, promises
effusive and broken, fossils that say we have
been here before and yearn to endure.

So hold me in the flickering night,
the firestorm that sweeps our mutilated earth,
deaf to the din of rabble rousers. Remember
how Elgar enveloped us in sublime enigmas,
how we sipped champagne from the Big Dipper
and thought we might float in galactic light.

Dear Hawthorn

A ferocious gust in a windstorm
cleaves the Hawthorn down its middle,
splits the concentric rings we've worn;
lean and opulent seasons of our being,
topples one-half onto the hillside
of yellowing knotweed behind the house.

And, I think of how one of us will fall,
the other left trembling in the wind, boughs
laden with moss draped like a shroud,
and its bounty of brilliant scarlet berries
where squirrels frolicked and squabbled, now

strewn over the ground. The living half
wounded to the depths of its Celtic heartwood,
bereft, as when Heloise was torn
from her Abelard, mutilated as the jagged
shards of wood left at the Hawthorn's cleft.

The half that endures, weary with grief,
awaiting the executioner's axe,
to leave, as in a severed limb,
the stump of its origin, knowing all
we were, and the roots that hold and hold.

The Pineapple Express

erupts like a Brahmin bull,
a high atmospheric river of wind and water,
bucking off corrugated roofs,
toppling power lines, whipsawing trees.
The sky gushing with the fury of it all.

Down here, we cower in our makeshift
dwellings like moles, wait breathlessly
for a mudslide to sweep us away, a tree
to crush us. Steps from orchard to beach
are swept like toothpicks out to sea.

We cling like survivors in Gericault's
Raft of the Medusa, defenseless in nature's
gnashing teeth. You awaken, screaming
the roof has fallen. Rats' eyes glower orange
in the dark, the rain pelts. I assure you

the rats have fled into the halls of Congress,
and are gnawing on the constitution, that we
have unleashed rampaging rivers of shame.
When the sky explodes in a solar firestorm
one sips Pina Coladas from a pineapple husk.

Did you know pineapples are a fruit
constructed of many berries, a collective
not unlike our species, before we split apart?
That their juice contains a corrosive enzyme
like vitriol flowing from senatorial mouths?

I'm just saying, let's bow down
to this iconic fruit that lives large in the minds
of meteorologists, can pair up with Spam
and melted cheese on a grilled bun, and trigger
bizarre metaphors in the grip of a tropical storm.

Life in the Balance

for Boris Brott
1944-2022

Dear childhood friend,
you blundered from a curb this morning
without a glance left or right,
and forfeited your life, sweet
and fragile as spun sugar. Left behind
tears bitter as horse-radish root.

You were the maestro, wielding a baton,
loved flamboyant bow-ties, Puccini
and Verdi operas, and you greet them now
in heaven's celestial orchestra. There are
no words to say or notes to play
to your beloved wife and children,
your brother who weeps on his cello,
to embrace this Coda that ends with a Finale.

We seek equipoise--a calm, joyous journey
along the balance beam of our lives,
unaware death hovers with beckoning arms.

Take, for example, one base pair substitution
in the double helix: seizures, blindness, low IQ.

A rogue wave that arrives without warning,
sweeps you away in a thunderous rush
leaving no trace in its crushing embrace.

The assassin dressed in a spiked coat
who suffocates your lungs and sends you
in a body bag to the morgue.

Why do we cling so mightily
to the inexorable onslaught of sorrow
that is to come? *Wobble, wobble* as a top
spins to its end, to lay itself down.
My old friend gone, never knowing
the last music from the last wave of his baton.

Yet & still,
our mechanic keeps the motor purring--
the eye never has its fill of seeing.

Skellig Michael

Say it was a problematic day—

The Ellie O'Leary bucks in crested waves
like a bronco spurred in the flanks,
diesel roaring with lift and fall of the swells
propelled from across the Atlantic.

Heave ho! Bile, sour as green apples,
pours from one woman, over the taffrail—
nothing closer to death than seasickness.
Other faces pale as ghosts.

Are we not all in the quest for ascetic revelations,
something to bring one closer to God? Here,
it's ascension—600 slippery steps hewn by hand
from granite, up to the beehive dwellings in the sky,
built by the blood and sweat of monks,1400 years ago.
A sheer wall looms, painted white as snow by guano,
the clamor of shearwaters, gannets and guillemots,
a deafening choir.

Too rough to land, declares Captain Decklan.
We protest: the monks did it in a curach,
made of tanned oxen hides stretched over pine ribs,
sealed with pitch, without a keel!

My eye roams up a green saddle of rock
to a helipad built for the filming of Star Wars,
Skywalker wielding a lightsaber.

Have we no shame in this resting place of the devout?
Perhaps the monks needed a Jedi master
to save them from the Viking onslaught.

Now, we've rounded the island's edge for home,
musings wafted away on the engine's smoke,
the fading cries of the rookery.
A thuggery of gulls mock our frailty.

Valentia Island Cottage in the Rain

You weep silently over a Binchy novel,
for a chubby girl named Benny, who has lost her father,
for your mother laid to rest a month ago.

A sleeting rain pounds the windows,
whips the red fescue into a frenzy in the meadow.
Across a finger of sea, mist cloaks Port Magee.
Black horses in the field huddle against the deluge.
I watch your red-rimmed eyes track death across the page,
ineluctable as the myriad headstones that pay homage
to this land's bloodstained past.

It is too much when you suddenly ask
what I want you to do, when I die.
Haven't given it much thought, I reply, a fist clenched
in my throat. Time for a walk. Outside, drops cling
to grass blades, dwarf Crocosmias dance in the breeze,
a slug indulges in a late afternoon snack.
The wind strums my ears, whispers, *Alive, alive!*

I hold you until the wracking sobs subside, 'till you are able
to gaze up into the light, and follow as I do now,
a white gull gliding effortlessly across the sky.

Backpack

The problem with a backpack is
stuffing it with too many things,

unloaded and loaded again, each step
of the journey, some items used only once,

others thrown away. A conundrum that seems
unavoidable, one becomes a beast of burden

like a camel staggering through the desert,
with a tent roped to its hump.

This results in a frenzy to reach camp, settle
before a panorama of snow-capped spires,

sipping Lapsang Suchong, wolfing down
buttered popcorn and sardines.

I can tell you there is satiety
in that kind of relief, so gut-felt,

it drives away the frigid night until dawn, when
you collapse the tent and buckle on the straps

of despair, saddled again with the painful
stones of progress along the trail.

You can measure this sort of enslavement
against the Galapagos tortoise,

which must shrug its thick carapace, miles
to find a succulent shrub. How we sacrifice

for succulence, proud of the onerous weight
on one's back—how much trail mix

and filtered water sloshing in the bottle, and
how far you can travel before the spine

accordions, how much surrender
before you let the boulder roll back down

the mountain. Sisyphus was not distracted
by regression linked to progress,

but it makes me want to weep—
that shining example of weightiness,

only love can lift. And when you say
this is too heavy, I cinch the straps tighter,

slog through scree on the mountain's flank,
carry home on my back like a hermit crab,

blunder like a blind bird
through a cloud forest to the peak.

It's all right to exult in the heavy lift,
an empty backpack at the summit.

To sniff the alpine flowers, and find solace
in the vespers of silence, to trust

you will ride on the shoulders of those
who know the way home.

The Cairn

I do not know who built this cairn
I pass each day beside the road,
five stones balanced precariously;
a gust of wind could knock them down.

I often stop to meditate
and ponder whose hands stacked these rocks
that glint like oil in the rain.
Once, one fell off, I placed it back,

lovingly and said a prayer
for children murdered far away,
and died a little more inside,
relieved the stone held fast next day.

Some bereft man, for his dog,
may have built this monument
or simply made a landmark here
to steer the lost ones on their way.

I do not know who built this cairn,
a heap of stones, in Gaelic tongue.
From it I learned the art of balance,
how hope endures when sorrow comes.

Rocky Mountaineer

We are herded aboard the Rocky Mountaineer
like sheep waiting to be shorn, 900 wealthy, souvenir
hunters jockeying for seats beneath the glass domes
of this blue and gold, diesel huffing pride
of Canadiana, where liquor flows like Yukon melt,
and canapes follow salted almonds, followed by
succulent beef and fowl in the dining car, if you please,
served by genuflecting mesdames & messieurs
responsive to every beck and call.

Shutters click in time to the clack of the rails;
broken bones and backs of the immigrants
who pounded the spikes that hold these tracks,
men who fell from the trestles, blown apart by dynamite
to carve out tunnels, and crushed by the rocks that fell,
long forgotten in unmarked communal graves.

Tall stands of larch flash by, laved golden in the light,
plunging waterfalls and jagged peaks, washed down
with another Bloody Mary, a platter of cheese.
Freight trains hauling logs and tar sand's oil lumber by—
an endless cavalcade of polluting black gold, bound
for the coast. No sign of the Salish or Chipewyan people
who fell like Vercingetorix when Caesar invaded Gaul.
Now, interred by the railroad moguls to profit from
one-armed bandits and roulette wheels in neon-lit casinos.
Wisdom of the forests, lakes and rivers, obsolete,
faded like memories of the elders.

By the end of the second day, grog blossoms appear
on cheeks as Banff beckons—a postage stamp town,
squeaky clean, turquoise waters of Moraine Lake, granite
towers of the grand Chateaus, overrun by the likes of us,
chattering and spilling popcorn, clicking selfies and texting—
reverence eclipsed by crassness, a Grizzly, nick-named,
The Boss, picking at garbage, and a chevron of geese flying
in the wrong direction. The pendulum swung too far
for the clock to reset time.

For the love of god, bring me another dram of scotch.

Hiroshima Peace Park, 2017

You would not know the provenance
of this rusted girder cupola,
passing by on the streetcar—
a stripped ribcage pointing its apex
to the sky,

so blue today—the park
with its monuments, fountains
and commemorative benches,
bean paste candy hawkers, and
stooped, white-haired women in black

who remember the solar burst,
the furnace, the parasol cloud,
wails of the burned and broken.
Bakeries, homes and hospitals
reduced to mountains of sticks.

Uranium, father of the Titans
left his lethal kiss buried
beneath the grass on which we stand,
last summer's leaves swirling
around our feet.

Standing in the shadow of the dome
laved in late afternoon sunlight,
you could not know the fury of the yellow-cake
atoms cleaved from their family, silent now,
as if nothing had ever happened here.

Great sorrow streams from the beaks
of addled crows, assaults our ears
in small explosions. A black feather
drifts down to mingle
with white petals that have fallen.

Icelandia

Our crampons bite deep into the glacier,
send ice chips that glint like zircons
skittering across Vatnajokull's face,
as we trudge mile after mile—Vikings
wielding ice-axes, clueless as to their use
should the need arise. One slip,

and you say, *we could die here,*
hurtling like a luge down the crazed
surface of this remnant from another age,
violently as sentenced men fall through
trap doors. The silence, devotional,
broken only by labored breath, the snap
of carabiners from fixed rope-to-rope,
sun setting the ice on fire,

the descent into earth's mausoleum.
Deep in this chamber you come close
to the world's heartbeat—
a long, slow rhythm. Light streams
through tectonic prisms casting blue
and silver jigsaw puzzles on the walls.
What I hope to see through a window
wavers in the darkened room—opacity
on the far side of the camera's shutter.

Formality envelops us stumbling back
in the dark. Headlamps, stilettos of light
to guide us across the ice. I could not say
in that hushed moment, looking back
from some imagined point,
how the austere splendor of that cavern
might shape my life, as we crossed
the river, on a pitch black night, to safety.

Nostalgia, Cannon Beach, 2018

At low tide the ocean
hollows out deep pools in the sand
where we splash and cavort
with our grandchildren, as in years
long past, when we sailed north
and dropped anchor in hidden coves,
and dove into clear green waters
with our daughters. Nostalgia hangs
like morning mist over the beach
as I recall the waterfall
at Tenedos Bay, where they fluttered
like shorebirds in the spray. Mornings,
we awakened to a congress
of ravens in the tall firs.

I am first to submerge
in the frigid pools, an old man hoping
to outgun his son-in-law, surface
like a submarine, spluttering,
to accolades from my wife and daughter—
I am the man! Beyond, the breakers roll in
as they always have, and blue spots dance
before my eyes. My granddaughter, Isabeau
looks at me, as if I were a manatee, then
prances into a shallow pool like a ballerina.
Griffin, my grandson, already brave,
dunks his head to retrieve a sand dollar.

All is caught up in this moment
of sheer delight, like the crest of a wave
backlit by the sun before it breaks.

Cannon Beach Sonnet

Where tufted puffins huddle on Haystack Rock,
and Pinion pines are bent by wind and time,
we walk together in the hungry tide
through shifting dunes and shells bleached white as chalk.

However harsh and transient life here,
will thrive as long as ocean is land's bride,
with all men's machinations set aside.
In our agedness the path's unclear.

We marvel at the complex rills that waves
have carved on sand when they spread over shore.
Above the rock, oystercatchers soar,
below we walk in footsteps of the brave.

If we must, like driftwood float away,
let our limbs be twined like hands that pray.

Piercing the Long Night

The Northern lights
rise like a kiss to the sea.
Arthur Rimbaud

I fall asleep on Iceland's frozen tundra
beneath a star-studded sky. Around me,
steam vents send ghostly wisps into the air,
roiling puddles of mud fueled by earth's crucible
simmer nearby. A band of horses huddled
in the distance, whicker softly, their manes tossed
like waves in wind. I stumble through a nightmare,

a beggar in a threadbare coat seeking salvation,
worn thin by years of pandemic, mayhem and murder,
the blood of children running in schoolyards.
Where are the angels we can entreat to prop us up,
puppets of our own making, to redeem our lives
so desperately short, to make us holy again?
Must they always hover, impassively out of reach,
flutter their wings in dismay as we fumble beauty away?

I awaken to a magical flurry of messengers from the sun,
a swirling swath of luminous green and violet rose lights
that sweeps like a wedding train across the sky, a sinuous belt
around the stars, embellishment of a kiss from the heavens
that pulls me back as dawn arrives over the world. I wake up
in a joymare to the sound of a voice come to take me home.

ACKNOWLEDGEMENTS

Earlier versions of these poems have appeared
in the following journals:

Steam Ticket 2020: Batman Lego
seems 52: Inviolable
seems 52: Hiroshima Peace Park, 2017
Evening Street Review 2020: On a Perspective of Things
Evening Street Review 2020: The Bones are Singing
Evening Street Review 2020: Election
Evening Street Review 2020: X-mas Heart String
The Halcyone Literary Review: Deep Freeze